# Serenity's Dream

A collection of tales and poems about mystical journeys.

*Cover image © by Brian Chase, 2006*

Printed in the United States of America

ISBN-13: 978-0615526133

ISBN-10: 0615526136

T.S.Garp

Acknowledgments


This is an acknowledgment to all the people that have been in my life, to music, themes, and authors that have inspired me to write, pursue, and create poetry that stretches the boundaries of my imagination. Creative dreamers we all are and I have been inspired by friends and family, Sara, Jennifer, Debbie, Kathy, and Tina, Music from the 60s and 70s, Reflections, Hope, The Moon and Stars, Dreams, Immortal Lovers, Forgiveness, Goddess of Creation, Fame, Sensuality, Fall Holidays, Sorrow, Nightmares, Mystical Adventures, Viking Lore, Mythology, Haiku poetry, The Deep Blue Sea, Devastation, Medieval Legends, Faith, Magic, Cosmic Journeys, Artist, Christian Riese Lassen, Moebius, Chris Foss, Ron Cobb, Picasso, Vincent van Gogh, Writers, Stan Rice, Oscar Wilde, Edgar Allan Poe, H.P. Lovecraft, Joseph Campbell, William Blake, Robert Frost, J.R.R. Tolkien, E. E. Cummings, Lewis Carroll, Emily Dickinson, Stephen Crane and J.K. Rowling.

A collection of tales and poems about mystical journeys.

Serenity's Dream

by

T.S.Garp

### *On the Road of Harmony*

A spring land being explored
How breathtaking
With shoes tied around my neck

Daylight of the sun
Westward wind, clouds gloom
Steal the view

In the afternoon,
The sapphire sky fused with the soil
Creating distant harmonies

A collection of tales and poems about mystical journeys.

## *Dark Skies & Roses*

The wind like a sharp knife was cut

Blew across her body rigid in plight

To the closed skies her watery eyes did open and shut

The adularia vastness of rapture gone apparently

In a set of roses clutched thorn blew apart despairingly

The tears flew on the wind and the rain dullness grew

That stayed heavy on her heart through and through

Like dying coals glowing red-orange in the sunset dew

T.S.Garp

## *All Hallow's Eve* (circa 1800's)


Orange-red pumpkin patches are in bloom
Birds chirp a song that autumn is here soon
The gray sky darkens, swirls and tumbles a windy gloom
The farmer will harvest one last time before winter's loom

Autumn leaves glowing red and yellow about
Foretells a winter coming for unlucky fellow with gout
Legends and dreams filled the air
Nightmares soon manifest without care

October has arrived this day, you see
Season of the dead and decay, take heed
So gather up all that you can from crops pulled by hand
From Summer's toil of the plentiful lands

Seasons yield safe from prying hands
By late autumn harvest plenty from dying lands
Kept that for storage during the long winter nights
Keeping vigil and warm by candlestick lights

Shudder and spook wail in the wind outside
Halloween begins in October's end to no surprise
Wishing November would reign in again
Leaving the departed ones cry out of pain and sin

When all settles down for the harvest feast come November's
end. Inviting neighbors, celebrating with friends, and consuming
turkey with kin. Faces and laughs not seen since September
Alive and well during this a long cold winter of December

A collection of tales and poems about mystical journeys.

### Neptune's Curse

The storm came powerful in the night
An ungodly wind sent forth from turmoil of Nott
It took us by surprise and shattered our flight
Casting doom upon our wondering wayward lot

Murky, dark-dreaded were they, thunderous clouds
Sirens singing a hiss of promise and gloom
Lightening silver-blue, blinding and screaming aloud
Serpents waiting underneath and striking with a boom

Neptune's curse set in motions
On lost souls who will not be found
Navigation was hindered by terrifying emotions
Massive waves come crashing down

Clashing wooden ships in a horrific sound
Sending many a man to Davy Jones' locker
Coral and reef, ancient ghosts chanting,
and echoing words to drown
Falling under, to a cold, death of water.

Terrible sea creatures of the depth
Serpents, kraken, hunting without rest
Murky, ancient doom, and blunder
Hideous bone crushing jaws of thunder

Down deep I go, wayward lost, pity soul
Some thing took hold of my misfortune,
Hands strong and soft, diverted me aloft
Pulling me up to breath again in such commotion

Hair of fire and eyes so blue
Once wicket creature of delight
She was the siren that held me true
Gives me life again anew in swirling seas of fright

## *Silver Sea Dreaming*

Dreaming, taking you by its toll

Unforgiving watching life slowly unfold

Riding on a silent storm above creation

Floating on an endless plateau of heaven

Shimmering, pools of glass

Vibrating waves, ripple and saunters past

Innocent sleepy slumber carrying me far at last

Protected by invisible, immeasurable, invincible loving care

Adrift in this silver sea made of hidden dreams of mine

Shape shifting, manifesting, visualizing, realizing

Moved by a breath of the slightest touch

Perfectly attuned with this universal drift so divine

Leading me to what is right and true

Leading me to you

I just close my eyes

And I arrive with ease,

without even trying too

A collection of tales and poems about mystical journeys.

### *The Long Voyage (Part One)*

The storm was great,
the long ship sailed safely passed the dire straits
The shadow of land could be seen in fog, and we spotted ghost
ships, wrecked in heaps embedded in bogs

By Odin's grace he watches over us
Proud of our Dragon-prowed ships, we fear nothing
Our hearts are rich. I shouted gleefully,
and say, this must be the way

For I am to go where no one has gone before
To set foot on some unknown sandy shore
It is not easy to leave, to leave my home,
and embark across endless seas and scribble in tomes

But I am the Viking King you see, I must not fall to my knees!
I must sail the oceans blue and conquer the lands
Pave the way for my clans. The Norsemen are here to stay
Let's stand and pray that we last each perilous day

But my thoughts give me away
For the future we make, from our hearts we create
Our world is vast and we must make it last
I've seen tribes and people of far, I wonder who they really are

Different and kind I've seen, very interesting
Not always war, but trade and more
I realize that the world is great and we should celebrate
Keep your mind open, eyes and ears clear (never fear)

T.S.Garp

## *The Long Voyage (Part Two)*

Keep your nose to the wind and embrace the good things in life
Enjoy the wondrous sights, love your wife, your children
Never fight and take this advice, from an old Viking King
I must travel the world and see what has not been seen

I believe we are destined to grow and learn and not be stern
Old age, can make you see a different way
Wisdom comes to you at odd times, but when it does,
it rings true and you never lose

The long voyage is never over, always seeking, always there
I sometimes wish it would bring me back home sooner
To snow covered land and taking my wife's hand
Drinking, eating, loving, and making babies every morning

I may be just an old warrior, been in combat too many times
Adorned with battled scars, hair white, and a face not too kind
But I tell you..... My heart is true. I have seen the light!
Finally! An essence of maturity! And by Odin! It is right.

I wish only peace right now, to all I meet
To be back home and surrounded by the sounds of my family
But I am stuck, obligated in this ritualistic formality
Destiny has put me in a long voyage to return, again

A collection of tales and poems about mystical journeys.

### *The Mystical Journey Express*

Come on! Join me on a trip to the sun
Ride this magical train and see the wonder and fun
Come on! Enchanted moment is waiting for you!
Get on board and let it take you away-don't delay!
Cone on! Bring all your friends too!
Let loose and let the journey begin today!

Go on! Have all that you can
Enjoy this instant, this life and the colorful land
Go on! Have the time of your life. It's all in your hands!
Make way! Grab all your friends. It's free!
Take them away over the mountains and across the sea
Make way! Cast off! I've got my ticket for this trip especially!

I'm ready to leave the station
Jump aboard and feel the joyful elation
Come on! See the world like never before
Just spread your wings and you will soar!
This magical moment is here for you and me
Let it take us far. Come on! With me and see the stars!

Let's go! Take a seat and have some fun!
Nothing is going stop our magical mystery run!
It's time to make our way across the velvet sky!
Let's go! Happiness comes from journeys far and wide!
Come on! Take a chance. Take a ride. Take a trip
Take time to experience this exquisite bliss!

It's all up to you, and me too!
Experiencing all the things that we do
Will shine in us and live it's life in you
So sit back, all and one, and enjoy the need
Hold hands, my dear friends, it's all fun
Make this bliss and enjoy the dazzling rainbow sun!

T.S.Garp

### *The Mermaid*

We met in the midnight hour
In the same place near the cemetery tower
Under the bright full moon during autumn's gloom
Near the seashore where lives were put to rest forever more

Far away from town,
we held our secret that must never be found
Guided by candlelight,
a luminous speck in the night

Over the hills and reef I tread carefully
All for my dearest,
overcome without dread confidently
From murky depths of water unseen

I could hear her sweet musical voice sing
Rising up to greet me instantly
A fair maiden so slenderly
Held me in her bosom so tenderly

Such bliss was this, my heart sang for you
To look upon glittering eyes and lips so true
To have love fancy me from the sea
A sweet kiss that held me passionately

A collection of tales and poems about mystical journeys.

### *The Gift of Nature*

During the autumnal

Woodland winds gust in pleasure

With plenty of leaves to blow


### *Dreamscape*

Dreams see us

When you close your eyes

Dreams come to us in the night

When all hope is gone

When you are on the last song

Dreams come to you so bright

In the deepest depth of your mind

Comes a clarity so fine

Dreams will remain and manifest in time

T.S.Garp

## *Star Bright Maker*

Stars so bright..........

Stars, twinkling in the night

I create them, I make them shine!

From twilight sky, I make a them mine!


Galaxies spiral out of the unknown among the souls

Nebulas outstretching beyond the limits of my control

Planets, stars, moons, all clustered together in the same room

With a wave of my supernatural hand, beyond time and space

I make the heavenly bodies come alive and bloom


Glowing red and blue, and soon all the colors too

Who am I? They call me by many names, they do

I am your Goddess of Love that helps you see it through

My dear creations stay, I behold the magical Milky Way!

A collection of tales and poems about mystical journeys.

## The Jabberwocky Writer

In that pleasant place I sit and wait
And watch the world drift in and out like pages
The days go by and I wonder why
As I hear the sound of air between the stairs

The blue over the moon under I sit, until the sun turns on
In a vast landscape of steel trees hidden in the mist
In a valley of roads that endlessly disappear
I write the chronicle echoing from my soul

Trekking through the route of common to visit the uncommon
I connect myself to the city and towns, and to the world
Yearning to express myself to be heard
Welling to go beyond the next step to reach the right word

## *The Artist*

Begins blank without a blotch
An idea comes from beholder with stretch cloth
Set in motion with great devotion
Taking care of thy creation with subtle emotion

Swirls tumble and fall
Colors mix and blend into all
Bright, dazzling, and dark
Lighthearted displays done for a lark

Artist push feather delicate and strong
Lays down dream of ethereal picture like a mystical song
With hundreds of strokes carefully orchestrated to desire
Capture images of joy and lament to set thy soul afire

Great rhapsody from admirers who stare in awe wonderment
Giving humble reverence of praise in deserving complement
Communicating and invoking tantalizing
Rejuvenating and mesmerizing

Precious is thee that arrange pigment and paint
Gifted young artists examination of spirits and saints
Beautiful compositions, complicated, and complete
Feed our hearts with motivation, memorabilia,
and melancholy is quite a feat

A collection of tales and poems about mystical journeys.

### *Reflections of My Soul*

Reflections of my soul,

passing through waves,

across an endless sea of tales, never told


Flowing of a sound remain

Echoing hearts linger on the brain


Mere shadows of the melody importunate

Departed true lovers, farewell unfortunate


Spurred by memories made so rarity

Reflections so despairing in a mist of uncharity

### Faces

Friendly faces fill my mind
Leaving  traces all the time

Lessons learned from every turn
Profound meaning that tells and yearns

Faces in the crowd some happy and some full of deprivation
Smiles trying to catch the sunlight of every expression

I feel their joy and painful sorrows
They want someone for all their tomorrows

I see people sit and think
Searching for that missing link

Bring us to that special place
Leaving this world without a trace

Every face tells an urgent story
Bright and wonderful they implore me

Dear lonely faces
In the tiptoe places

Share your dreams with me and clear them
We can sheath them in gold and endear them

Faces I see.......
Fill my mind and never leave me

Maybe this time.......
Maybe in the rhythm of my mind.....

Traces......
Faces........

15

A collection of tales and poems about mystical journeys.

## *Japan Horizon*

Across the waters over thousands of miles

Leaving home on wings of steel to follow the setting sun

Embarking on a journey to that faraway place

Traveling to the Orient beyond the horizon

Arriving on the shore of the Land of the Rising Sun

Neon glitter, colorful displays, dazzlingly the eyes and senses

Perching noble dragons and lions of red and green

To ancient serene countryside full of tradition

Soothing spiritual gardens, ponds, lush greens and pink trees

Clearly a foreigner I partake in such, sushi, sake, and sumo

Visiting mysterious destinations both old and new

Drifting through the cafés and art galleries of Shimokitazawa

Extraordinary technology and ancient culture clash

Mixed with sublime reverence and utter shyness

So many exotic people with great hospitality and smiles abound

To my happy destination at Osaka with a single pleasant sound!

Exotic faces, politeness, and clean pristine places make me stay

T.S.Garp

## *Midnight Dreams (Part One)*

In the shadow of night
On a boat sailing by satellite
I was below deck, trying to sleep
Not realizing the ship has struck a reef

The crew scrambled topside, but I remained inside
I heard screams in a dream
And I awake to find myself alone
Lifeboats gone, had the crew abundant me, and gone home

The fog lifted and I could suddenly see
An island shimmering out into the sea
The boat pushed forward by crashing waves
The surf sending the wreck deep into a cave

I saw human bones all around
I wanted to scream but I may no sound!
I jumped, leaped, to the rocks below
I ran for my life, I was never slow

To the jungle where I saw a light
A mansion, a beacon in the middle of the night
I rapped on the massive wooden doors
Hoping that someone had seen me from the sandy shore

The door opened and a pale face greeted me
Violet eyes, she was oddly beautiful and kind,
long dark luxurious hair and without hesitation,
gave me a hug so tight, I said: I'm cold and confused

A collection of tales and poems about mystical journeys.

## *Midnight Dreams (Part Two)*

Taking me out of the gloom, she sat me by the burning fire
Forgetting my prior doom, and she removed her revealing attire
Wrapping me in a wool blanket of comfort she whispered:
"I taste the joys of life and give you freely my powers of sight."

Bewitching me a kiss on trembled freezing lips from icy waves
Torturing and mocking me, she insanely laughed upon graves
Realizing too late: What have you done? My ship? My crew?
She smiled with eyes hypnotic and wise, a kind of witches brew

I knew. For I was doomed to be here for a thousand years
Broken, trapped delightfully on an island full of sailor's tears
A mere token held softly, captured by a Siren's bliss……
Beguiled and tricked, I was forever in love by her deadly kiss

### *Buena Vista of Heaven*


On the top of the world
I lay down to touch
As sky and ground merge rumbling

Icy blue vista
Delicate white frozen crystals
Delightfully melting in liquid pools

Radiant purity of land
Soft fingerprints laid
Upon a frigid world just made

A collection of tales and poems about mystical journeys.

### *Into This World (Part One)*

I came into this world from someplace before
My mind wasn't clear; I was lost in thought
And not sure, I didn't know where I was
I only knew that I needed to find love
and my home was miles and miles above

From colors of blue-white-and gold
I arrive onto a landscape green and so far ahead
The sounds filled my head of nature and life
And I knew the answers were waiting for me instead

I traveled on under the tallest trees
Watched sunbeams danced and gleamed
I walked silently for many miles it seems
I found my image flowing in a stream

I didn't know where I was at this moment in time
The smell of flowers filled the air and they began to shine
I've seen so many new things, so sudden like a dream
I followed the windy-worn path of a life made seen

I came to this place decorated with style and taste
I found a town full of people, wishing and singing
I saw her there, Sakari, pretty and mild, moving with such grace
I heard their dreams coming from their words left lingering

Not shy at all they greeted me with open arms
She came over to me, unafraid, and took my hands
Eyes gleaming gray pools beheld me so much,
That spoke of love like endless crystal sparks in sand

T.S.Garp

## *Into This World (Part Two)*

To the Valley of the Ancient Ones
We departed this crowd
She led me across the hills traveling many miles
Past deep forest and darkening clouds

She came into this world for me
She said she had been waiting to see
She pressed her body close to mine, I would never be sad
She brushed away tears of joy and was glad

She had the power to hold me tantalized
I smile at the truth of this divine and realized
This was meant to be, I came into this world for thee
I fell from the sky on a beam of light to find this life!

We live in the temple of eternity and our hearts of gold
Timeless as rocks and air, immortals we are never getting old
She keeps close to me with deep green eyes forever seeing
Our love growing over the centuries, outlasting mortal beings

We ponder and watched the World of Man return to the sea
Nothing was left but an ocean of sadness and insanity
Despair, but the world came back, from tumble and fall
Merciful, leftover saved from an Ark of Humanity

Mistaken for Gods, eons ago, luminous beings who saw
Caretakers and Admirers of this world, made hope law
Immortals' dreams and faith it seems did create by day
From a gift of love from above, after all, they say

A collection of tales and poems about mystical journeys.

## Minerva's Magic

She took me by surprise, this petite witch
As she walked in the room holding the candlelight
Her voice sensuous as she sung a tantalizing song
Breathing out words to me in the middle of the night

Mysterious and beautiful she was in the tavern low-lit glow
Never had I seen such a women as this, she was so graceful
Smelling of something sweet, a mischievous sparkle in her eyes
She didn't say anything, except give me a kiss to my surprise

Like a dream slowing manifesting
Her eyes so blue and hair beyond fair were offerings
Her smile was bewitching, cute and devious
And she had set her sights on thee, quite delirious

Long after that my mind was perplexed
All that I could think about was her no less
We quickly departed Salem and headed out west
We were married, happy, and never had time to catch our breath

Minerva cooked with a cauldron of massive size
She held an hourglass and spices and herbs with pride
She possessed a rickety broom and she howled at the moon
All and all, my wife could work magic, and I was her groom

### *Tombs in the Mist*

The wind blows brisk
Across the mar landscape
Comes a heavy mist

Blackened trees naked
Twisted, the dead forest
Surrounded by the spirits of the wicked

Ancient tombs long forgotten
Filled with the unrest
Haunting ghost from the gloom long dead

A collection of tales and poems about mystical journeys.

### *Fallen Starlet (Part One)*

*Your still pretty baby.......*

The time was so long ago
When you were younger than now
In a place far away in the land of lights and play
You screamed out aloud!

*Your still pretty baby.......*

You moved to the city
You had to get out of this place
You got off that airplane and said, "I'm ready"
You left the scene without a trace

*Your still pretty baby.......*

5 years ago you hit New York and LA
You let nothing stand in your way or trust!
You were gonna make the grade
Stomping on Hollywood you push back all their lust!

*Your still pretty baby.......*

You became a Big Star baby
Everybody wants to be you
Can you still come out and play?
They ask, "What kind of tricks can you do?"

## *Fallen Starlet (Part Two)*

*Your still pretty baby…….*

10 years gone, you became a singer-movie star overnight
At the top of the world there was nothing you couldn't do
But like love made too soon, the joy fell out of sight
This fickle-glitter town turn it's back on you

*Your still pretty baby…….*

20 years down the road and your fans have left you
Time has not been kind, no one is holding the door or way
Nothing to do, you want to leave it all behind, feeling so blue
No more golden globes or praise, you don't want to stay

*Your still pretty baby…….*

But that was 30 years ago yesterday!
You find yourself in Vegas working one bright sunny day!
You hear new fans screaming out your name
You have come full circle all the way

*Your still pretty baby…….!*

A collection of tales and poems about mystical journeys.

### *Summer Rituals*

Watching them trek across the sand

Hot underfoot from grains sparkling like tiny glass

Seeking and venturing new places to dwell

Planting a symbolic flag of right

Settling in an open house without walls

Lingering for just a minute before running

Toward the blue crystalline massive pool of water

Cooling themselves from the summer heat

Repeating this many times

As the ladies watch from the shore tanning themselves

### *The Moon (Part One)*

She heard it all before
The Moon

Will soon
Sing it's tune

And the night will cease it's nocturnal gloom
The tiny flowers will start to bloom

And she will ride the broom
Fly to see her tragic groom

See him there under the cold tomb
Gliding down from the dark clouds

Cast a spell
Near the well

Make a Luna wish
For the love who was sick

Recreate that life
Make it real tonight

Drawing in the stars so bright
Watch it burn

And see it turn
Come home and wait

Do not hesitate
Your love will arrive

A collection of tales and poems about mystical journeys.

## *The Moon (Part Two)*

By candle light
To your surprise

A witches' curse has set things right
Knobs and broomsticks

Cauldron and fire
Have made your desire

Return with passion
There, under the burning pile

Watch the dust form
Into life once more

The lost loving souls will rise tonight
Dead lovers, vastly departed

Across the dead sea of time,
Return from their eternal resting light.

Wait one hour and see
What you have long desired to be

Rap, rap, rap. Hear the knock on the door
And get ready to meet all that you have made of lore

For dreams and nightmares ring true this night
Your lover returns with a fright......... good-night

T.S.Garp

## *The Lonely Mr. Immortal Who*


I have seen the world spin into oblivion
I have seen the sky darken and turned cold
I have seen all the storms that haunt men's souls
I will be there at the End of the known Universe
I will watch the time slip away once again

There are no limits or bounds for me, no end
There is nothing that I can not do or conceive in
There is no place in time I have not seen or been in
There are some places better left alone and forgotten

My time machine and I are infinite, past, present, future
My glory, my curse, my triumph, my gift, my reality
My eyes have witness galaxies and civilizations now dead
My life immortal through time and space, and with that said

I am the last of my kind, a time traveler without a name or face
I came from Lords of Wisdom who's story is known and told
I no longer have friends who can outlast from getting old
I am alone, simply searching, just to rest for a peaceful place

A collection of tales and poems about mystical journeys.

### *The Terminator Takes California*

Listen to my plan
I am the new man
I am the one to set things right
I have the might

I was created from the future
To come back and correct the mistakes made by losers
I will terminate all oppositions
My rules will be obeyed without your decision

Come with me if you want to live
Join my forces like some others did
We must break them down
Bring new order to this town

No room for evil politicians
I will fix the tax laws without their permission
I never drink water, I'm made of skin and metal I am boasting
Our government needs to hit the gym,
and stop all that girly-man wine toasting

Give me a target and I will fight
I have infrared vision and can see you at night
No matter what Skynet does or the Gov
I will conquer them from above

Cyber-technology will do the rest
I will blast them with speeches and take no less
The state of California has always been rich
And I was created to battle for it

The deficit is mark for liquidation
I was designed to see its final termination
But as Governor I need funds to see it done
Damn, this job is not so fun

### The Journey

In ancient land
Many smiling visitors travel
Happily overwhelmed with astonishment

### Winter's Dream

Icy tundra cracks
Frigid dreamer stirs awaken
From this frozen December day

### The Excited One

Blinding-
Elation's scream
Penetrates the sunshine

### Ocean of Serenity

An enchanted sea voyage
Sailing over the great saturated expanse
Mesmerizing the senses following the wind

A collection of tales and poems about mystical journeys.

## Devastation and Hope

Coming in a wave of fright
Coming in the dead of night

Earth shattered in two
Earth crying for you

Oceans boiling-swirling a deep crimson blue
Oceans unkind rushing in to swallow you

Nature gone mad
Nature tormented and sad

Shaking a hectic dance
Shaking terrible all across the land

Pray for hope, Pray for life
Pray that everything will be all right

Give us strength dear God like a mighty sword
Gives us courage enough to live once more

Be our savor this night,
and days to come

Be our guiding light,
and let us bath under the peaceful sun

Give us hope and faith to last us through
Once more

T.S.Garp

## *Tibetan Journey by Way of Sky Train*


A beautiful place to visit, left me departing tears
Colorful dreamy country full of smiles and cheers

Braving the *Sky Train* to reach heaven and my lost soul
Alongside mystical snow covered mountains of old

Greeting me hundreds of times with friendly dark eyes
In traditional dance of beaming happy faces making new ties

The women wearing their gold and silver amulets ran in twos
Proudly trekking across vast landscapes delighting us, they knew

Clad in rainbow garments silently showing their dimples
Gently taking my hand guiding me to snow-peaks,
and mar temples

Inviting me to sit in their homes and take a sip of their wine
Entrenched festival gathering joyful laughter filled my mind

Awaking the next day in an spiritual oasis lost in another time
My Tibetan journey, humble, reverence,
lay upon me a peaceful shine

A collection of tales and poems about mystical journeys.

### *Over the Hills and Far Away*

Venturing deep in the forest hidden from sight and sin
Concealed from those misguided who might wonder in

Guided by challenges, knowledge, and heaven's hand from afar
She adorned herself with the amulet of her divine star

For only Apprentices and Learners who knew had merit
Clad in their green cloak of wisdom they have inherit

She had dark raven hair and a face of an angel that define
Her husky voice, though sweet and delicate a sound is thine

Hearing the whisper of the wind so pleasant and true was a sign
Birds singing in the morning dew she knew this was the time

Bold, beautiful, brave, and bare underneath she had no need
Taking on this courageous mystical journey without heed

She moved through the woods, deliberate, graceful walk
Traveling silently, humbly, in tuned without talk

She gave praise to the benign elemental spirits this hour
Her arms outstretched embracing all of loving nature's power

Giving thanks and respect to the ancient lore that hid
Worshiping the trees and mountains on this journey that bid

Over the hills, through the wilderness, she called out: mine
Taking on this spiritual quest to reach the secret shrine

Moving stealthily under the play of stars like a fairy in the night!
Across the landscape, terrestrial angel, dancing in the daylight!

### The Time is Right

When the girls start dancing, when the wine starts pouring
When the people begin to talk and say: I am having a good time
The time is right, when the neighbor's dog quiets down
When sleep takes control and your off and dreaming
When you think, all you ever had is all you will ever need

*The Time is Better*

When that special person you like, likes you even more
When time will let you say, hey, it is going to be okay
When they will take your hand, off on a walk to a peaceful place
The time is better, when you can go out, make it, and even think
you can. When the nymph of your dreams come to you in
everlasting beauty.

*The Time is Best*

At night, when all you can think about is the everlasting light of
good cheer. The spring loving and the autumn leaves falling. The
time is best, when you are with a large group of friends, sharing
old memories, ideas, and the best of times. When you are talking
alone with the person, you especially want to be with. When life,
love, beauty, and friendship mean the most to you

*The Time is right!*

A collection of tales and poems about mystical journeys.

## *Behind the Mirror of Addiction*

I can't stop staring at my image in this window of tricks
I can't hide how I feel with wounds that bleed with salty licks

Black and blue, I want to break away and just be
Feeling like a fool, I want to runaway and leave me

Whenever I walk into this town without eyes to see
Whenever I talk to clowns without numbers to reach me

Feeling trapped behind these grubby walls. Why don't they
make me believe? Is it hopeless? Waiting for me to fall

Eerie distorted shadows dancing down the hall
Communication breakdown, silent messengers won't call

I got myself to blame for all the problems on my list
I stare back into the mirror of the woman who made this

Dark circles under the eyes, I want to leave the image of me
Dreadful appearance I must somehow face this and see

I have to cover my scars, fix these tears in the mirror that stay
I have to shatter this dire look and kick these fears away

Begin again with a new face, a new gaze to set my soul free
She was pretty once and now she stares back with such a need

Nothing, no one, nor myself is going to get past my sights
I will change, make it right, and not give in without a fight!

Come on, Self and Will, and face me, dare to make it bright
I'm no longer waiting, I'm ready to begin a new life in the light!

## *Heritage of the Quest (Part One)*

*The Medieval Sages of Tristan McKlue*

Tristan McKlue:
This is how it starts, I hope you like this part!
When I was young, I had the power to dream,
that I could do anything that no one had ever seen
I knew the land, the air, the waters, held no fear for me

I never asked how it was sent, they were my friends. I played
with nature and never asked what it all meant. For I had insight,
hope, fear, joy, longing…. The ever-present wanting.  I was alone
there most of the time, keeping people back behind the line

Time past, I grew, became aware, saw the power of other
people so happy without despair. I learned, I read, listened to the
wisdom the ages had to spare. Inspired, I live again, giving my
best in hopes that the world around me can past the test. Alone I
must, but not forever, for such a journey is better when your
together with the right woman…so ever!

A collection of tales and poems about mystical journeys.

## *Heritage of the Quest (Part Two)*

### *The Medieval Sages of Tristan McKlue*

Tristan McKlue: (This is part two)
Greetings dear reader or whomever reads my log
book. I leave for the quest, let no dragon or peril slow me to rest I
shall take a fair maiden who will accompany me through
tranquility, and together we will seek a land to our prosperity

The stranger (me) rode into town, people there called it Vansella,
an oasis surrounded by rugged mountain ranges, and dense
forest. Not many travelers come this way, any that do are soon
on their way......again. The outsider sparked new curiosity, every
human eye seem to be upon him, I should know, they were
looking at me, Tristan, the explorer and apparent oddity

I informed the local gentry that I was of good standing, and our
conversation was amiable. I expressed I needed a strong young
woman as a wife and partner in my exploration of wonder

The journey will be an adventure, in our memories and hearts,
and ring in our mind years later like thunder. Who would join me?
A former knight of the War of Druids, a trader of skins and
common goods, a traveler searching for a proper home after this
mystical quest is over and to sing and laugh of our deeds done

## Heritage of the Quest (Part Three)

*The Medieval Sages of Tristan McKlue*

Tristan McKlue:
Good morning to you! I am impressed with this place, Vansella. I appreciate the care and kindness the people have given me, but now I must leave. After settling down for a day and a half, rested, fed, washed, traded, gold in my pocket, supplies bought.

The Elders escorted me to the center of town, where groups of families gathered, and pushed in the front, there were teenagers and women in the lot of age sixteen to twenty. They were diverse, from near peasant girl to craftsman's daughter, they were blonde and brunette and smelled of a sweet scent, wearing their best outfits, dresses, smocks, and some had on flowers

Oval pretty eyes watched me, some were very dark, while others had blue, green and gray too, and I didn't know what to do. The were well proportioned, happy, giggling young nymphs, slender short and tall, and they were all waiting for my approval or hint

I didn't expect any dowries, such as land, rent, loose furniture from these women, however so, the families were most anxious to find husbands for their available daughters. I approached them preparing a speech that would either encourage them or sway them. When done, I will wait yonder

A collection of tales and poems about mystical journeys.

## *Heritage of the Quest (Part Four)*

*The Medieval Sages of Tristan McKlue*

Tristan McKlue:
The months have past, and I am at last, a happy man on the
right path. The land to the North we made carefully, encountered
castles, kingdoms, even sat by fire and converse with wizards
who warned of demons. But magic was on our side, call it luck
from where gods shine, for Virginia was my bride! In retrospect, I
remember the day that faith presented me her good company

In Vansella, I had requested an interview with four, separately I
walked with each, and we talked some more. Almost in an
instant, their silent souls spoke to me, and I knew which one it
had to be! Virginia was her name. Her long blonde hair, eyes soft
and bright blue, and she was tall too, a gentle smile, and a laugh
that tickled my heart, the others were pleasant and nice enough
but they lack that, how should I say, that certain kind of stuff

The genuine brilliance she had was all powerful. Nature yielded
to her in such a way, to send flowers floating in the air from
a cool breeze on a bright sunny day. When I became direct, her
answers were correct, and true. Thus, Virginia dashed off, for
she knew it too..... To buy a new dress in the middle of this
Why? For the long venturous trek, of course. She is delightfully
mysterious, a free spirit, a woman of heart, a true lover of art

T.S.Garp

## *Heritage of the Quest (Part Five)*

*The Medieval Sages of Tristan McKlue*

Virginia McKlue:
Dear reader, hello, how are you this find day? This is my turn, I
have something to say. My husband has all the fun, writing down
in his weather-beaten log book, from winter to summer, keeping
a record account of our interesting travels in our world of wonder

He writes in poem-script, and I love him for it. I want to, too
Though I am hesitant to convey my whole history, for I am shy,
and my man, this darling man next to me, may blush openly, at
my kinds of thoughts. I will write it out secretly for thee.....

Day by day and season to season we shall say. But he knows
me already, from best friend to husband. My mind is in tangent
with his thoughts and my heart beckons for the voyage that we
are undertaking together and saving a record to last forever

You dear reader, have not heard from me before. So we begin as
friends in written form. About Tristan, this love of mine for two
years calling, we go through the seasons and unknown realms
listening to the songs of our lives. Braving the world underneath
our traveling feet and welcoming all that we meet

We are one, he and I, and we share many things and do not lie.
The gods call this bounding of a spiritual kind, indeed, they say
it's older than time. I am so glad he found me there. My life at
that time was bare. From wishes I made in the night, he came on
request. I am proud to be part of the heritage of the quest!

41

A collection of tales and poems about mystical journeys.

### *The Path of the Valkyries*

They can see the frozen sunlight
Where there is no life
Bold and beautiful in the deepest night

Across frozen lands and frontiers
From some distant shores beyond Nordic seas
Riding the tundra in hopes of finding Valhalla

Venture forth chosen few
Glory awaits those who are true
By Freyja grace if stumble and fall
Rest assured in tumble of battle when Odin calls

Let the gilded Gates of Adgard sooth the heart
Travels majestic make heroes and kings
Wise old sages make legendary dreams
Who makes haste to aid the final glory of Ragnarok!

### Finding Clarity from Disillusionment: A Journey

Ups and downs, confusion spinning you around

Feeling like you're trapped in a merry-go-round

How many lessons learned before you can discern?

When will I attain the peace of mind,

that comes from wisdom in time?

Brightening, uplifting my soul and wandering mind

Making clear and giving me hope for a better time

Forever learning our life flows and undulates,

and knowledge comes to those who wait

For all life is a journey and we must hold steadfast

Storms come and pass, but we will last

A collection of tales and poems about mystical journeys.

### *Moonlight Enchantress*

I see her dancing in every glade, day and night
She lives underneath the stars and baths in the moonlight

Taking no mind or heed of anyone that comes by
Her graceful body, so sure, she takes each step precisely

Catching my eyes on her, she slows her midnight dance for me
She than beckons me to come near and dares me to see clearly

Unable to resist this enchantress. She takes hold of my hands
and says to thee: Your are so handsome, you like to watch me?

Wearing only a white gown like some angel of the night
She said to me: Can't you see and hear the four winds sing?

I listened and to my surprise I could hear a distant orchestra,
sweet music begin to raise. Her voice, gentle from rosy lips

She sings along too, guiding me through each step of the music
Dancing, she and I, naked and free, under the moonlight's eye

T.S.Garp

## *Driving Through the Storm*

I found myself on that long, widening road, under a million orbs
The day was reckless, lifeless, and I saw no hope or home
This world bringing me down and a hot storm came to wash
away the haze, no retrieve, only added to the sorrow I had obtain

I drove on wondering where I was going, not sure this was love
How could it be like this and have no end in sight or light
A teenager's dream and dilemma, I road into the night,
not knowing which way to go, was there any hope from above

Heading down that dark highway of lost dreams, til morning
Going as fast I can go, without stopping, running away
Not knowing if I would ever get back home, on a road, pitch
black. Nothing guiding me, except headlights, and faith this day

My life is a mystery and I'm not sure where I am going tonight!
I need to see a new life, a better one, where I can be just me
Nothing seems to make sense, clouds fill my mind, and
I want to leave it all behind, on my way, I got to find the light!

A collection of tales and poems about mystical journeys.

## Voyage on the Sea of Dreams: How I Met You So Many Yesterdays Ago

Let me take you back to that special day when we met
We were sailing along on that sea of dreams for so long
On a ship made of steel, we had said hello and our pleasant
journey began slow. In the shadow of love we spoke that song

Many years ago, riding on the ocean blue, over the waves with
you. During that holiday voyage, watching the ocean sunset
come in, gently spending the time together, and than you knew
That I loved you! The years rolled on and now we're here again

Remember, laughing and loving with you, so young and bold,
and how I dove into the deep ocean for thee, and found a black
peal under some seaweed. Presented it to you, my dearest, how
you cooed. Come with me, my love of dreams, back to the sea

Intrepid sailboat take us back there, embrace the wind, and see
Steering us to where the palm trees sway in the breeze.
Anchoring, disembarking, island of love. Barefoot, laughing--
talking-walking, white sand crossing, eyes reflecting in the sun

Come with me and imagine how it used to be, my love. Let's sail
on that voyage of dreams from yesterdays. Exploring the world
to find paradise, to a destination on that sandy horizon of ours
Let us run across the shore to see our dreams unfold, again

Take hold of my hands, now confident from a life wiser and
strong. A lifelong journey meant to find you darling, like a song
Our beautiful Windjammer stood restless as the wind blows
eagerly. Laughing, we would not leave this paradise so easily

T.S.Garp

## *The Playwright*

Moving the pen forward ever so by touch
Lay down a perfect scribe as best as much

Contemplate, work your fingers to the bone
Deliberate, try to come up with that simple tone

And if you see the world that you want to have
Never stop wondering if it can be done, just laugh

A shinning crown of fame on the run is not the task
Writing a good piece of literature and dramatic play that last

And if see you the miles ahead of you start to pile
Do not hinder, welcome them with open arms and a smile

Your solitary goals are to move forward and reach the sky
Ignore watchful vacant eyes who keep asking why

From harsh, heartless critics that may say: You can't do it
From rude naysayers who sabotage, trying to ruin it

Time, nor the hour, will not stop this roller coaster ride
This delicate life will push onward to the end of the tide

With a simple stroke of the pen, from an idea its seems
Fully visualized, an ink blot began from late-night dreams

You move up and around disbelievers, and make a stand
Let thy creation come through naturally from your hand

Write a masterpiece full of words of wonder deep into the night
Spinning a yarn full of drama and plight by candlelight!

Manifest what's in your heart and soul to behold
Create a play that will be worthy of work that's retold

A collection of tales and poems about mystical journeys.

### The Bob Dylan Perspective
### (Political Satire of the 1960s)

Sitting here singing a song, like Bob Dylan had done
Trying to understand right from wrong, up all night until dawn
With eyes younger and strong, from the next generation
I am not waiting and pondering for very long, I bring Revelation

The times are a changing, a new voice in the White House
The Man, he is rearranging, laws and rules, cheese for a mouse
Let us not bow down, as the police state grows. Let us not
praised this clown, stealing our Social Security as we grow old

Leave the 60s behind, wait for the 70s, 80s, and 90s to arrive
Leave all the bad signs, survive the next wave, and being alive
Rise up my friends with freedom's love! Give them a flower!
Take your lady's hand and give her a white dove! Feel the power!

Don't mess around with Johnny Slim! Turn the fight to them!
The world is a crumbling to the sea, better learn how to swim!
Open your eyes! Only love my friends is the answer and the way
No surprise! Learn to forgive and build a bridge, to save the day

Look out folks, make a stand, the future of us is going to shout!
Be a tower of our strength, make them believe without a doubt!
21$^{st}$ Century com'n! Believe the Lord of Legend will fix it tonight
Time is run'n! Better make sure people, you help to get it right

So sing along with me, and tell them we just want to be!
Take my hand friends and you will see, just how they tease!
Revolution, save our Constitution, we need a better solution!
No more politicians, backward institutions, create a better
resolution for you and me!

T.S.Garp

## *The Stars in Your Eyes*

The stars shining,

as you walk by.

A heavenly gleam in your eyes

A collection of tales and poems about mystical journeys.

### *Emily is Light Years From Home*

Emily awoke with a single thought: What happen to me so
suddenly? A beam of light came down and struck me so coldly
Where am I? My head is spinning so full of commotion
The last thing I remember, I was swimming in the blue ocean

She found herself alone and her confused thoughts started to
roam. She was in a low lit room surrounded by eyes of the
unknown. Strange machines glowing oddly in the dark, flickering
lights of red-green-yellow-blue, seem to be humming loudly

Strange voices inside her head, speaking to her directly. Telling
her to relax: We are taking you away for a special task
They say matter-of-factly: This how it's done, since the dawning
of your sun. Just sit back, take this ride, and enjoy the fun

Emily was stunned-shocked, but she wasn't afraid so much,
even when they told her that she was 100,000 light years from
home. From a port window, Earth left behind in a sea of stars
blazing-glittering, across the cosmos to another world, with trust

Calming and soothing, alien thoughts explained to her to stay:
That's good, don't be frighten, confused, or try to run away
Emily knew that they were merely taking her to new home
Why? she asked. So that you would no longer feel alone or sad

The alien spacecraft landed on a planet's coastline. It's gleaming
surface, smooth as glass, and looked like paradise. Emily stood
upon purple sand, happily watching the red sun, yellow-green
glowing sky. Emily saw living twirling rainbows and wanted to cry

A wondrous world so beautiful and sought, 100,000 light years
beyond any dream, she thought. Creatures of energy-light, they
say: It's alright dear, your home! Glowing living spheres, kind
aliens, welcoming her to this place, Emily now calls her own!

T.S.Garp

### *Thunderstorm in the Wilderness*

Coming like a sound of  thunder over the meadows

Sparking a light so white made of fire

Through the air without stopping


Making no sound when striking a blow

Broken and crooked it went unheeded

Powerful and clean, it does burn so


Lonely silhouette sentinel standing in the night

Landing down upon an unlucky wayward soul

Ancient living force could light up the night with fright


Hoping that silent, bolt, from storms that bring life

Wishing for rain, yin and yang, befalls death on dark clouds

A mighty gleam, white-blue ray that makes a clashing sound

A collection of tales and poems about mystical journeys.

### *The Past of Them in Chapters Lost*

Can you, see blue skies from chapters lost
Can you, wish the pain away from that high cost

Will it make you sad or make you smile, you want to  run
Contemplate, on past dreams was it all said and done

Did you forget those dreams, so many tears
Wait, was it lost in that rage, old feelings that sear

Neglected, was it such a long time ago to your dismay
Planets spin, were you the same as you are today

The clock ticks, can you make the old times return
Take a step back, to visit an old journey to learn

Was it all said and done, so long ago back than
Did you remember that journey's song, my friends

How I wish their sound, to see them near to me now
Old friends of the past, so dear, left under dying clouds

T.S.Garp

## Happening on That Thursday Afternoon

I'm just beginning to fine. Now I'm on my way
Nothing matters to me. I'm just chasing the clouds away

Somewhere far and dear. Something calls out to me
The sky is drawing me near. I wonder why

Such pleasant voices I hear. Reaching out and telling me why
With a heavy sigh. As I soar across the heavens waving bye

Looking at my reflection. Over the blue ocean shine
Just the kind of day to leave it all behind

Gracefully swaying to the music of love
I wish you could come with me and see

This beautiful day above, so true
On this Thursday afternoon! Wish I could spend it with you!

This Thursday afternoon, I'm just beginning to realize
Now I'm on my way. Nothing matters to me this day

I'm just chasing these clouds away
Somewhere far and dear. Something calls out to me

The sky is drawing me near. I keeping asking why, feeling so shy
Such pleasant voices I hear. Reaching out and telling me why

I soon realize with a heavy sigh!
As I soar across the heavens waving good-bye!

A collection of tales and poems about mystical journeys.

### *The Sad Watcher*

From that which the window seer gazes

Looking out at the world moving in slow-motion

Held deep inside a metal box designed to go

Wondering……..

A view from above as life rumbles a silent dance

Hundreds of people, blank faces in every direction

The sad watcher, isolated, observes all of this

Just stares as if in a trance

Wondering……..

## Where is Home

Sailing down from that strange place
Leaving your body behind
Forgetting the time...

Somehow the reasons are clear
You have been waiting so long
Searching for that door...

Wanting for somebody to say where
Looking for that smile to take you home
But you are exhausted...

The changing years roll by like a sad song
Where is that key to your heart
And you find it there...

With words of a different song
Where your soul is so happy to be
A gentle path to home...

After searching for so long to be
You suddenly realize that which you need
A true love to call your own...

Welcome home!

A collection of tales and poems about mystical journeys.

## *Green Skies*

Soaring beyond the horizon

Past the valley below

Through the piney forest

Over the shore and lakes of old

Gliding up to reach the green skies!

T.S.Garp

## *The Celestial City*

A glowing astrid cityscape

Rigid and soft, metallic and plastic

Rich and poor, huddled near the shore

Spiny towers twinkle and multiply

From the tiniest dweller a silent move

Impressive and deceptive appearance

Grandeur beyond belief and beautiful

A timeless place set under the night sky

Mimicking the sparkle of the starts

The city evokes a defiant stance against all

No shudder of thunder is greater than this

Silent sentinel burgeoning across the sea

A collection of tales and poems about mystical journeys.

### *Run To The Sun*

Like the wind you rise from dust

Reaching out to the world you see

Through the longest time of your life

Feeling the wind of the day like eternity


Have you looked up at the sky, never asking why

Have you seen the wide open spaces making you run

Across the bright horizon of our mornings we fly

Wishing to gather speed, trying to reach the fallen sun


Have you seen the light of the moon change color

Have you seen the stars glittering so far and wonder

Across the misty sky, soaring looking down at the ground

Going to a distant place, you know not what you have found


You want to run to the sun tomorrow

With wings of love that never dies leaving sorrow

Created from heaven, wondering is all life myth and lore

You ask yourself on the way to the sun: Have I been here before